Rocky Mountain Wildlife

Includes:

Rocky Mountain Biomes

Habitats and Habits

Bird Activities

Mammal Activities

Reptile & Amphibian Activities

Invertebrate Activities

Wildlife Respect

Waterford Press

www.waterfordpress.com

Introduction

The Rocky Mountains of North America include three major biomes—montane, subalpine and alpine tundra. A biome is a large region that has similar plants, animals and organisms that have adapted to the geography and climate of that area. A biome can have several ecosystems.

An ecosystem is a community of organisms that interact with each other and with their environment. Several ecosystems can exist within a biome. Ecosystems within the three major biomes of the Rocky Mountains include rivers, open meadows, forests, mountain lakes, wetlands and riparian areas (riverbanks and lands next to streams).

A diverse range of animals live in the Rocky Mountains, including the black bear, snowshoe hare, woodpecker, mule deer, elk, pika and yellow-bellied marmot.

Rocky Mountain Biomes

Montane

The montane biome of the Rocky Mountains ranges from 5,000 to 9,500 feet. Large ponderosa pines grow on dry slopes, with grasses, herbs and shrubs growing between them. Habitats include rivers, streams, lakes and open meadows, with a colorful array of wildflowers growing there during the summer. The quaking aspen and Douglas-fir grow in this biome, as do the mountain iris and plains prickly pear cactus. Golden eagles and mountain bluebirds are some of the birds that inhabit this area. Mammals include elk, bobcat, and mule deer.

Subalpine

The subalpine extends from 9,000 to 11,000 feet, just below the tree line. Forests of evergreen trees, mountain lakes and lush fields of colorful wildflowers provide habitat for many animals like the coyote, mountain lion and yellow-bellied marmot. The subalpine biome receives a higher amount of precipitation than the montane or alpine biomes, with snowfall accumulation sometimes five feet or higher during the colder months.

Alpine Tundra

The area above 11,000 feet, known as "the land above the trees," is called the alpine tundra. With strong winds and very cold temperatures, many plants and trees that grow at lower elevations do not exist here. Moss-like cushion plants exist by "hugging" the ground to avoid harsh winds. Other plants, like the alpine sunflower, have "hairy" stems and leaves that protect them from wind. Others have red pigments that can convert sunlight into heat. Some animals that have adapted to life in this cold, snowy environment are the white-tailed ptarmigan and bighorn sheep.

Class Act

Animals can be sorted into categories based on certain characteristics. The system for sorting animals into categories is called taxonomy. Mammals, birds, fish, reptiles and amphibians belong to a class of animals called vertebrates. Vertebrates are animals with backbones. Invertebrates are another class of animals that do not have backbones (like insects, worms and spiders).

Draw a line between the mountain animal and its class.

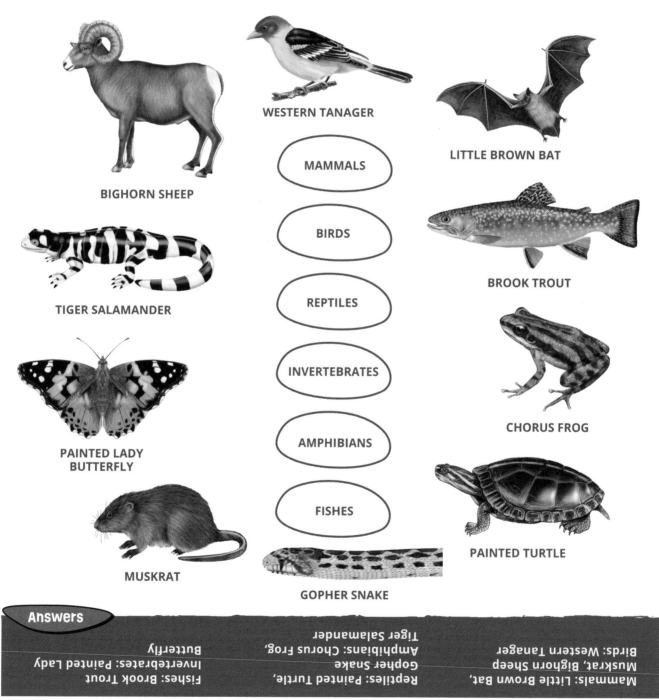

WESTERN TANAGER

LITTLE BROWN BAT

BIGHORN SHEEP

MAMMALS

BIRDS

REPTILES

INVERTEBRATES

AMPHIBIANS

FISHES

TIGER SALAMANDER

BROOK TROUT

PAINTED LADY BUTTERFLY

CHORUS FROG

MUSKRAT

GOPHER SNAKE

PAINTED TURTLE

You Are What You Eat

Herbivores eat mostly plants. Carnivores eat other animals.
Omnivores eat plants and animals.

Draw a line between the animal and its diet.

WOOD DUCK

WOLF

OMNIVORE

MOOSE

PORCUPINE

HERBIVORE

RACCOON

STRIPED SKUNK

CARNIVORE

MINK

LYNX

Food Chain

A food chain is the order in which animals feed on other plants or animals.

Producers – A producer takes the sun's energy and stores it as food.

Consumers – A consumer feeds on other living things to get energy. Consumers can include herbivores, carnivores and omnivores.

Decomposers – A decomposer consumes waste and dead organisms for energy.

Label each living organism below as a producer, consumer or decomposer.

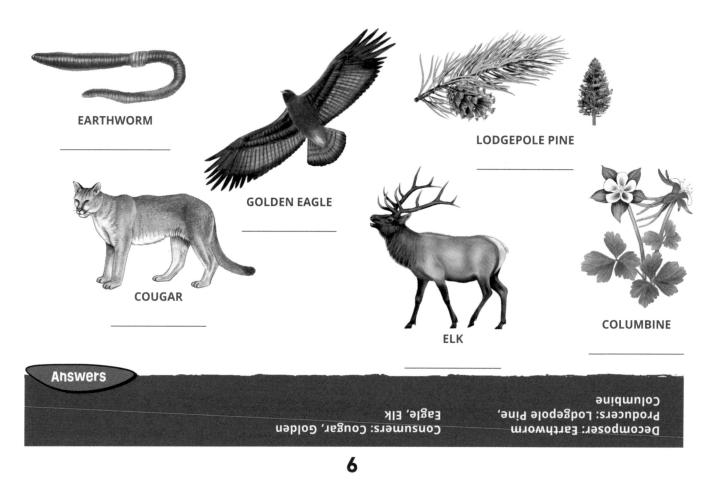

EARTHWORM

_____

GOLDEN EAGLE

_____

COUGAR

_____

LODGEPOLE PINE

_____

ELK

_____

COLUMBINE

_____

Picture Scramble

Place the numbers 1 through 9 in the lettered boxes
on the right to create the image on the left.

BLUE GROUSE

1.	2.	3.
4.	5.	6.
7.	8.	9.

A	B	C
D	E **3**	F
G	H	I

BOBCAT

	2.	
1.	3.	
4. 5.	6.	
7. 8.	9.	

A	B	C
D	E **1**	F
G	H	I

**RED-NAPED
SAPSUCKER**

1.	2.	3.
4.	5.	6.
7.	8.	9.

A	B	C
D	E **4**	F
G	H	I

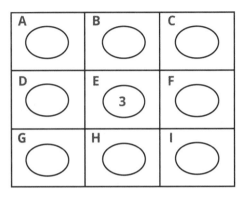

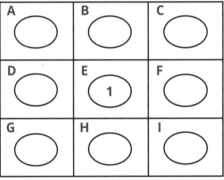

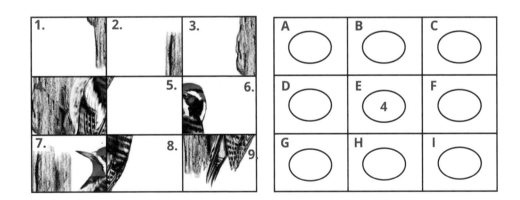

7

Word Search

Nearly 300 bird species live in the Rocky Mountains. Many of them live in the montane biome due to the lower elevation and milder conditions. Others, like the common raven and white-tailed ptarmigan, have adapted to living in colder temperatures at higher elevations.

Find the names of these Rocky Mountain birds.

```
S  N  A  Y  J  S  E  C  J  L  J  R  C  Y  D  C
E  A  T  A  N  J  T  L  T  Y  A  A  H  J  D  T
S  S  C  A  A  J  O  C  C  A  S  E  O  U  H  A
T  T  A  A  T  N  N  A  T  J  N  E  V  A  R  D
A  R  E  T  N  A  N  A  E  T  J  G  A  C  A  D
L  O  E  L  G  A  E  N  E  D  L  O  G  A  L  N
S  L  Y  K  L  A  D  R  R  D  E  N  N  H  G  A
J  T  A  J  C  E  J  A  E  A  C  L  C  A  C  G
N  H  A  E  L  A  R  A  J  G  L  T  G  A  E  T
E  N  J  C  O  N  R  S  T  A  A  A  D  C  S  R
A  R  E  D  T  C  G  C  J  H  Y  N  T  T  E  J
J  E  Y  A  R  A  N  H  T  A  A  E  A  A  C  E
A  L  A  N  A  N  J  U  N  U  Y  N  J  T  S  K
E  A  J  C  L  T  N  T  J  A  N  A  T  A  L  G
V  Y  R  T  R  N  N  T  N  Y  R  A  N  J  D  A
A  N  A  N  R  E  N  E  T  O  A  S  G  O  O  T
```

GOLDEN EAGLE

NUTHATCH

STELLER'S JAY

CANADA JAY

TANAGER

JUNCO

Answers

RAVEN

NUTCRACKER

Be An Artist

Draw this bird by copying it one square at a time.

The **common raven** is a large black bird found throughout the Rocky Mountain region. It is distinguished from the similar American crow by its large size, its large, broad beak and its call, which is a horse croak as opposed to a distinct—*caw*. Ravens are among the most intelligent bird species and are capable of remarkable feats of problem-solving. They are revered for their intelligence and spirit by many cultures.

Color Key

Color Me

The **western tanager** is usually seen in forest openings in the Rocky Mountains during the summer. It travels south to Mexico and Central America during the winter. It gets its red face from a pigment in its diet, which most likely comes from insects that get the pigment from plants.

Color this image of a western tanager.

Color Key

Word Search

All North American mammals give birth to live young that feed on milk from their mother. Mammals are sometimes secretive and difficult to spot in the field. Some, like the mule deer, are often seen browsing before dawn in open, shrubby areas but will seek cover among trees during the day.

Find the names of these Rocky Mountain mammals.

PORCUPINE

```
Q O Y G C L A A G D E H W Z M N
V A Z W D X M B B V H S L Q H J
O D R B S A S M L F J O X T I N
M M M M R Y K Z A K M F G H N R
B F C J U F U X C R E Z H E O E
H L I V M S N Q K F M P G G J D
F X B L W Y K L B J P O I P Q S
Y J K E N A X R E D I R T A P Q
C G D A A P M I A Z K C S N B U
L J R V J V M L R T A U V E P I
S Y E J F Q E C U H M P M D O R
S T E O Z Q D R X V I I H N L R
S N D T B B O J Q R X N N D S E
F B I K H K P S H H S E X C M L
C G C L M S U H X C E W P W C I
R B L W I J H L Q G J D X D P R
```

PIKA

RED SQUIRREL

MARMOT

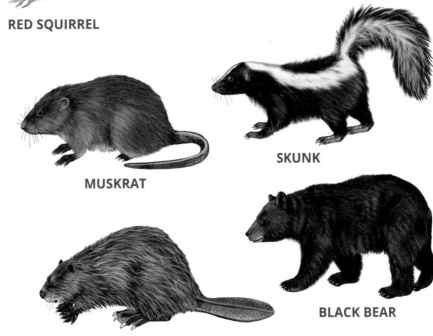

MUSKRAT

SKUNK

BEAVER

BLACK BEAR

Make Words

The **yellow-bellied marmot** is a large rodent that lives in alpine areas of the Rockies. A social animal, it lives in groups of up to several dozen individuals. When the colony forages in meadows for food, one or two individuals stand guard over the troop. If danger approaches, the guards will whistle loudly, causing the group to retreat underground to the safety of their burrows.

How many words can you make from the letters in its name?

_____ _____

_____ _____

_____ _____

_____ _____

_____ _____

_____ _____

_____ _____

Origami

Several species of bats live in the Rocky Mountains and serve an important role in the ecosystem. Bats pollinate plants and help disperse seeds, and they also help control populations of insects like mosquitoes.

Starting with a square piece of paper, follow the folding instructions below to create a bat.

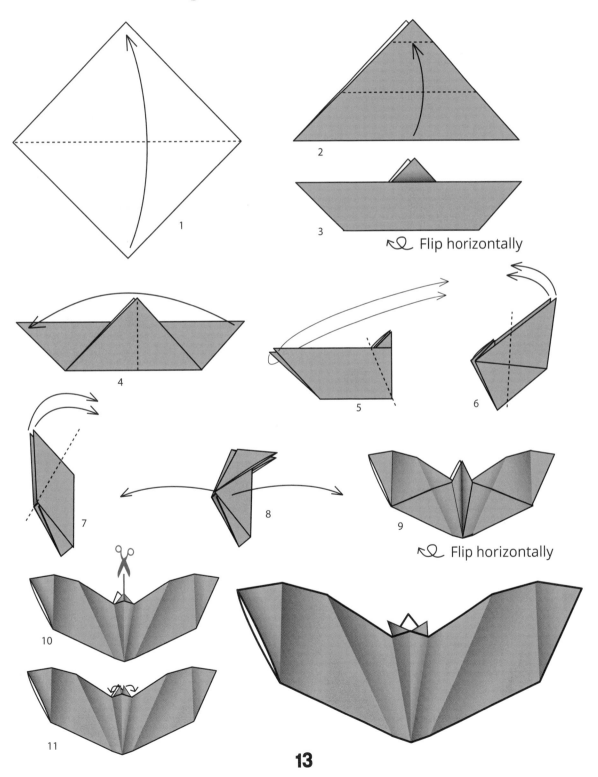

Word Search

Find the names of these Rocky Mountain predators
(animals who prey on other living things).

GRIZZLY

COUGAR

WOLF

RED FOX

RIVER OTTER

WOLVERINE

WEASEL

MINK

P C D U B U B Y C R M B M W A E
I U G C Z J S G J Z E W E R X S
H R N F I W Y Q C W D D X Q P P
N H I Y I E B Q D O O J F Q M H
X U X V W S V H C L U V Y O O S
N D Y Q E U V N X V X G X Z X F
C F H R A R B Y F E K R A J X N
B M W V S F O Q Y R H I J R A X
F F N O E A E T W I S Z M B D M
L C Q D L N V N T N J Z V M I P
J L F C O F H K H E M L R W V H
F E R B A G I L Y X R Y B F S M
J X X H L P Q G A L O A N O S I
I O B J E L N Y B O B X L X F N
X J F O P R N D S E M S Q C B K
Z H I R R Y S M A G K X Q W W Y

Answers

14

Connect the Dots

The **grizzly bear** is an apex predator, which means it is at the top of the food chain. It has a distinctive hump on its back, which is actually a huge muscle.

Follow the numbers to draw a grizzly as it catches salmon in a mountain stream.

Maze

The **striped skunk** is one of the most common and widespread North American mammals. They are often smelled before they are seen since they exude an unpleasant odor. When threated, they spray aggressors with a foul liquid that is so unpleasant that many predators like foxes, wolves and cougars do not hunt them. A true omnivore, it eats a wide variety of plants and animals.

Help the skunk find something to eat

ENTER

Animal Tracks

Studying tracks is an easy way to discover the kinds of mammals found in an area.

Draw a line between the Rocky Mountain mammal and its tracks.

CHIPMUNK
I have light tracks with four toes on my front feet and five toes on my back feet.

BEAVER
My tracks are unusual because in soft mud you can see the webbing between my toes.

GRAY WOLF
I have tracks like a pet dog, with four toes on each foot, and my claws always show.

1.

2.

3.

4.

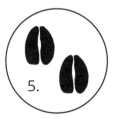
5.

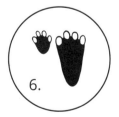
6.

COUGAR
My tracks have rounded toes, and my claws don't show because they are retracted when I walk.

ELK
Like most hoofed animals, my tracks have two long toes that make up my track.

SNOWSHOE HARE
I have long back feet and short front feet. All my feet have four toes. I am named for my large back feet that help me move through deep snow.

Be An Artist

Draw this mammal by copying it one square at a time.

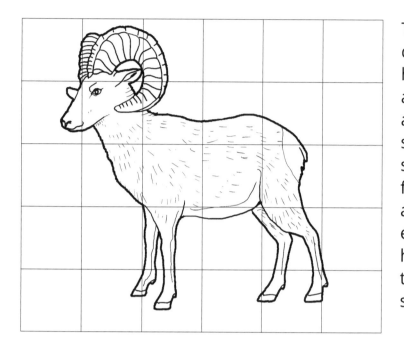

The **bighorn sheep** is distinguished by its huge curling horns. It lives in high mountain areas and has special hooves adapted to stick to rocks like suction cups. During breeding season the males compete for females by rushing at each other and smashing their horns into each other. For this reason, males have specially adapted skulls so they don't get injured by head-smashing.

Color Key

Make Words

The **black bear** is common throughout the Rocky Mountains. Its coat color is usually black, but in the northern Rockies cinnamon and brown bears are also common. A true omnivore, it feeds on a variety of plants and animals, but it is mostly a vegetarian. The black bear is easily distinguished from its more dangerous cousin, the grizzly, by its snout, which is straight in profile. Grizzlies have a more concave or "dished" face.

How many words can you make from the letters in its name?

Origami

The snowshoe hare and Nuttall's cottontail (also called mountain cottontail) are two types of rabbits that live in the Rocky Mountains. The snowshoe hare is aptly named because it uses its hind feet as "showshoes" to help it move on top of snow.

Starting with a square piece of paper, follow the folding instructions below to make a rabbit.

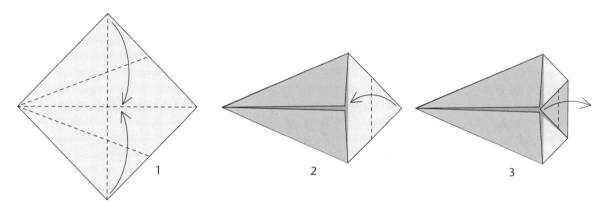

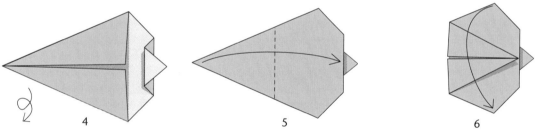

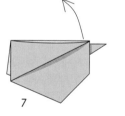

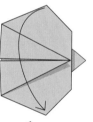

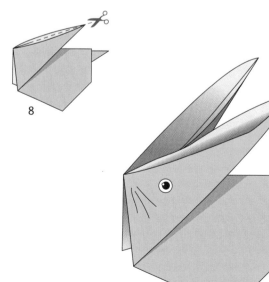

Crossword

Use the clues for Rocky Mountain mammals to solve the puzzle.

ACROSS

2. Another name for a cougar (2 words).

4. "Crazy like a _ _ _."

6. Bunny with big feet (2 words).

7. Dam builder.

9. Makes "bugling" calls during mating season.

10. Hunts in packs.

11. _ _ _ _ _ _ _ _ goat.

DOWN

1. Named for its large curled horns.

5. Biggest bear in the Rockies.

2. Deer named for its huge ears (2 words).

8. Also known as reindeer.

3. Large weasel.

Answers

Connect the Dots

Follow the numbers to connect the dots and reveal a mountain mammal that is known for its huge size and massive horns.

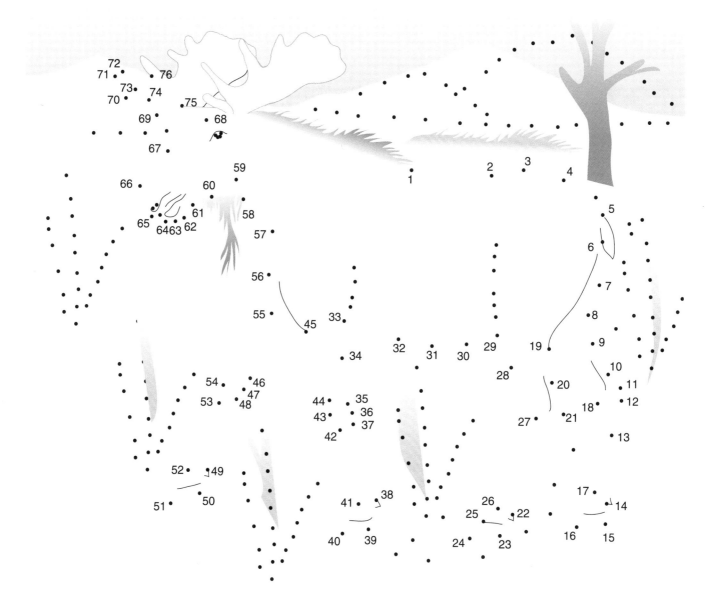

Make Words

The **badger** is a fossorial animal. "Fossorial" means it is adapted to digging and lives mostly underground. It uses its long, front claws to dig in the ground to make a burrow and uses its back legs to kick out the dirt. It is known to dig faster than any mammal, including a man with a shovel. A badger  usually dens in shallow burrows except during breeding season, when it will dig a nest chamber deep below the ground. The badger's black feet each have five toes. The front feet have long, thick claws an inch or more in length. It has small eyes and ears and a slightly pointed nose. Its keen sense of smell is second only to that of members of the dog family.

How many words can you make from the letters in its name?

_____   _____

_____   _____

_____   _____

_____   _____

_____   _____

_____   _____

_____   _____

_____   _____

Answers

Possible words include: badge, barge, beard, grade, bread, aged, bead, bear, dare, dear, drag, drab, gear, grab, rage, read, bag, bed, beg, gab, rad, dab, are

23

Word Search

Find the names of these Rocky Mountain fishes.

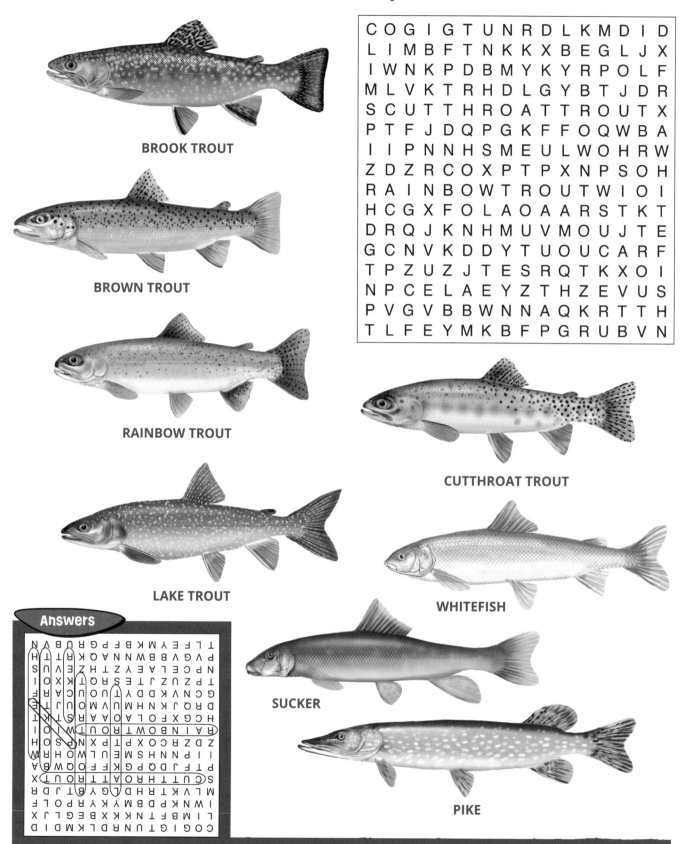

BROOK TROUT

BROWN TROUT

RAINBOW TROUT

LAKE TROUT

CUTTHROAT TROUT

WHITEFISH

SUCKER

PIKE

C O G I G T U N R D L K M D I D
L I M B F T N K K X B E G L J X
I W N K P D B M Y K Y R P O L F
M L V K T R H D L G Y B T J D R
S C U T T H R O A T T R O U T X
P T F J D Q P G K F F O Q W B A
I I P N N H S M E U L W O H R W
Z D Z R C O X P T P X N P S O H
R A I N B O W T R O U T W I O I
H C G X F O L A O A A R S T K T
D R Q J K N H M U V M O U J T E
G C N V K D D Y T U O U C A R F
T P Z U Z J T E S R Q T K X O I
N P C E L A E Y Z T H Z E V U S
P V G V B B W N N A Q K R T T H
T L F E Y M K B F P G R U B V N

Answers

Maze

The **western tiger salamander** is also sometimes called the "mole salamander" because it spends most of its time underground. The tiger salamander digs its own burrow, unlike other salamanders, but will sometimes use the burrow of another animal like a pocket gopher or ground squirrel. A tiger salamander can live 10 to 16 years!

Help the tiger salamander find its burrow.

Connect the Dots

Amphibians are smooth-skinned, limbed vertebrates that live in moist habitats and breathe through lungs, skin, gills or a combination of all three. Most reproduce by laying eggs in or near water. The endangered boreal toad is an amphibian that used to be common in montane habitats of the southern Rocky Mountains. Unfortunately, its numbers have declined, possibly due to a fungal infection but also due to loss of habitat.

Connect the dots to draw a warty toad on its lily pad.

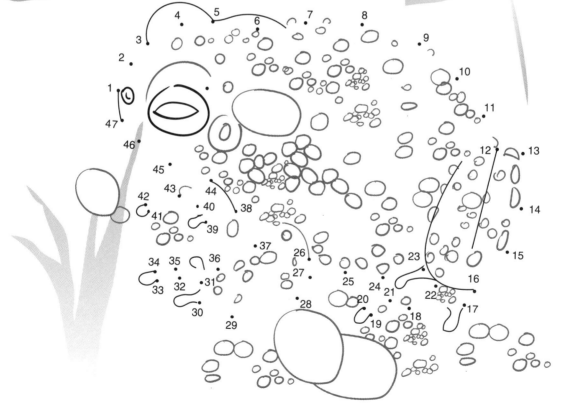

Word Search

Find the names of these Rocky Mountain butterflies.

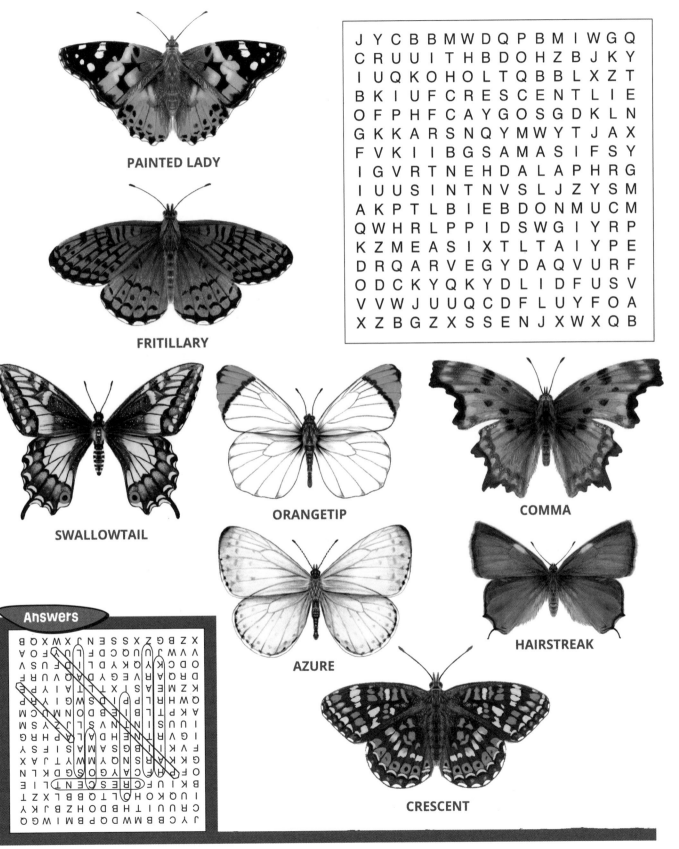

PAINTED LADY

FRITILLARY

```
J Y C B B M W D Q P B M I W G Q
C R U U I T H B D O H Z B J K Y
I U Q K O H O L T Q B B L X Z T
B K I U F C R E S C E N T L I E
O F P H F C A Y G O S G D K L N
G K K A R S N Q Y M W Y T J A X
F V K I I B G S A M A S I F S Y
I G V R T N E H D A L A P H R G
I U U S I N T N V S L J Z Y S M
A K P T L B I E B D O N M U C M
Q W H R L P P I D S W G I Y R P
K Z M E A S I X T L T A I Y P E
D R Q A R V E G Y D A Q V U R F
O D C K Y Q K Y D L I D F U S V
V V W J U U Q C D F L U Y F O A
X Z B G Z X S S E N J X W X Q B
```

SWALLOWTAIL

ORANGETIP

COMMA

AZURE

HAIRSTREAK

CRESCENT

Answers

27

Color Me

Dozens of species of butterflies live in the Rocky Mountains. In fact, 141 confirmed species are found in Rocky Mountain National Park! The **anise swallowtail** is a large butterfly that can live at elevations up to 14,000 feet and is commonly spotted in the Rocky Mountains.

Color this image of an anise swallowtail.

Color Key

Butterflies and Moths

The two groups differ in several ways:

Butterflies	Moths

Butterflies
- Active by day
- Brightly colored
- Thin body
- Rests with wings held erect over its back
- Antennae are thin and thickened at the tip

Moths
- Active at night
- Most are dull colored
- Stout body
- Rests with wings folded, tent-like, over its back
- Antennae are usually thicker and often feathery

All butterflies and moths have a complex life cycle consisting of four developmental stages.

1. Eggs
2. Caterpillars (larvae)
3. Pupae (chrysalis/ cocoon)
4. Adult

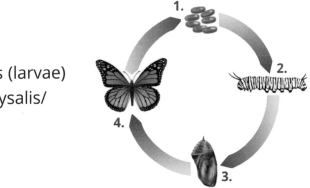

Attracting Butterflies to Your Yard

Food – Almost all butterfly caterpillars eat plants; adult butterflies feed almost only on plant nectar. Your library or local garden shop will have information on which plants attract which species.

Water – Soak the soil in your garden or sandy areas to create puddles. These provide a source of water and minerals.

Rocks – Put large flat rocks in sunny areas. Butterflies will gather there to spread their wings and warm up.

Brush – Small brush piles and hollow logs provide ideal places for butterflies to lay their eggs and hibernate over the winter.

Who Am I?

Insects represent 60% of all life on Earth and are a very important part of the animal kingdom. Many insects of the Rocky Mountains, like the monarch, leave the mountains for warmer climates during the winter. Others, like ants and ladybugs, huddle in large numbers to stay warm.

Draw a line between the Rocky Mountain insect and its name.

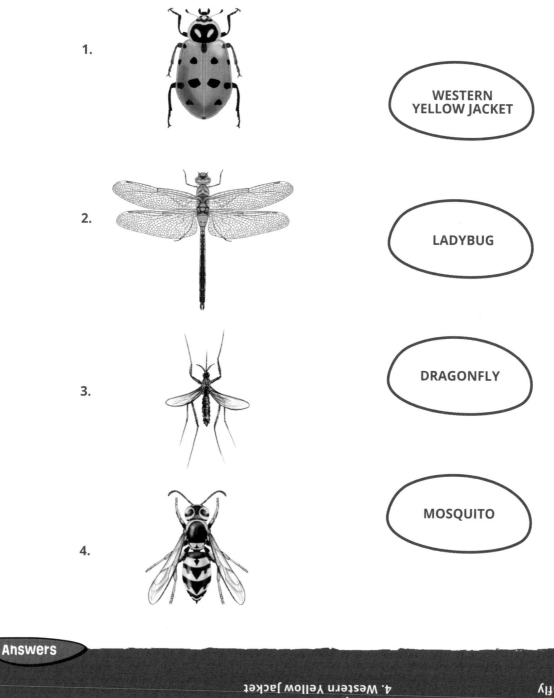

1.

WESTERN YELLOW JACKET

2.

LADYBUG

DRAGONFLY

3.

MOSQUITO

4.

Name Match

The Rocky Mountains are home to more than 5,000 plant species, including hundreds of species of wildflowers. Some of the plants have colorful names that describe them.

Draw a line from the plant on the left to its description on the right.

1.

COTTON GRASS

A. Found in both the montane and alpine biomes during the summer, each flower on this plant resembles a small elephant head with ear flaps and a trunk.

2.

HEARTLEAF ARNICA

B. This plant has yellow flowers and heart-shaped leaves. It grows in dry montane and subalpine forests.

3.

ELEPHANT'S HEAD

C. This plant grows in the Rocky Mountains in subalpine wetlands. It has slender leaves and tufts of fluffy, cotton-like fibers that help disperse its seeds.

4.

MOUSE-EAR CHICKWEED

D. Each of this flower's white petals split almost in two, resembling mouse ears. It blooms in montane meadows and low alpine zones.

Wildlife Respect

In wild spaces, humans are the visitors. We are lucky to be able to observe animals in their natural habitats. Along with that privilege, comes a responsibility to respect the animals we see, as well as their homes. The best way to learn about wildlife is by quietly watching. Though the possibility of getting a better look—or a better photo—can be tempting, getting too close can be stressful to a wild animal.

Here are some ways you can help reduce the number of disruptive human encounters that wild animals experience:

1. Know the site before you go.

2. When taking photos, do not use a flash, which can disturb animals.

3. Give animals room to move and act naturally.

4. Visit after breakfast and before dinner when wild animals are less active.

5. Do not touch or disturb the animals.

6. Do not feed the animals.

7. Store your food and take your trash with you.

8. Read and respect signs.

9. Do not make quick movements or loud noises.

10. Report any encounters with dangerous animals.